Growing in Joy

Growing in Joy

31 meditations
for a life in abundance

Robert F. Morneau

New City Press
Hyde Park, New York

Published in the United States by New City Press
202 Cardinal Rd., Hyde Park, NY 12538
www.newcitypress.com
©2006 Robert F. Morneau

First published in 1998 by Saint Mary's Press, Winona, MN

Cover design by Durva Correia

Library of Congress Cataloging-in-Publication Data:
Morneau, Robert F., 1938-
   Growing in Joy : meditations for a life in abundance / Robert F.
   Morneau.
         p. cm.
   ISBN-13: 978-1-56548-244-9 (alk. paper)
   ISBN-10: 1-56548-244-1 (alk. paper)
1. Joy--Religious aspects--Christianity. I. Title.
   BV4647.J68M67 2006
   242--dc22
                                          2006005479

Printed in the United States of America

Contents

Introduction

I have seen joy. I've seen it on playgrounds where children are lost in glorious play, in a mother's smile as she embraces her newborn baby, in a teacher as the seniors cross the stage to receive their diplomas, in the signing of a contract after months of intense negotiation. I've experienced joy on soft autumn evenings when the moon hung low and burning leaves told of distant things, when news arrived of the home team's victory at a regional tournament, when the surgery of a friend was successful and health returned.

Joy, the Virtue

Joy is more than an effect, it is also a cause, a patterned, disciplined action that when habitual, is a virtue. Here is my one sentence definition: The virtue of joy is a habitual action that leads to the enlargement of life for oneself and others in that its expansive energies give us zest in living and hope in dying. This longer description finds its grounding in a shorter description found in the etymology of joy. The word "joy" comes from the Latin word *gaudere*, meaning to rejoice. Both "joy" and "rejoice" are defined by phrases like "to gladden," "to delight in," "to take great pleasure."

As Georges Bernanos states in his classic *The Diary of a Country Priest:* "Joy! A kind of pride, a gaiety, an absurd hope, entirely carnal, the carnal form of hope, I think, is what they call joy." Hope takes flesh in the virtue of joy.

William Blake, the metaphysical poet, tells us in his poem "The Little Black Boy" that joy is an action. His phrase is "And round the tent of God like lambs we joy." Joy is a way of leaning into life. It is a consistent activity that brings light or delight to the journey.

The transcendentalist philosopher Ralph Waldo Emerson provides another explanation about why joy is a virtue and not just an effect of good, moral living. He states, "They, too, believe that where there is no enjoyment of life there can be no vigor and art in speech or thought; that your merry heart goes all the way, your sad one tires in a mile." Joy gives vigor, zest, and art to civilization. It is a virtue because its energy for life leads to good.

Looking at Joy

What does the virtue of joy look like in a person? My portrait of a joyful person includes at least four characteristics: presence, creativity, acceptance, and enthusiasm.

Presence. Joyful persons consistently exercise the grace of presence. Practicing the art of presence takes tremendous energy and discipline (read "virtue"). When we surmount the walls of loneliness and separation to take delight in the company of our loved ones, we know the marvelous intimacy that comes from joy. Through meditation and contemplation, joyful persons consciously take delight and pleasure in the presence of people and events. Such attention gives life.

Our loving God is present in all things, at all times. We can only enjoy when we are present to God in whatever circumstances we find ourselves. The spiritual journey is a mixture of both joy and affliction. Jesus knew the high excitement of the wedding feast of Cana as well as the agony in the garden of Gethsemane. What was essential was the presence of his Abba in both instances. The suffering became tolerable by the deep down delight in the sure presence of God. This was made possible by the virtue of joy that brought the beloved to consciousness.

Thea Bowman, a Franciscan sister, was a well-known lecturer, singer, teacher, and preacher. Even as she lived with terminal cancer, Thea inspired thousands of people with her joy. Not long before she died, she told an interviewer for *U.S. Catholic:*

> I don't make sense of [suffering]. I try to make sense of life. I try to keep myself open to people and to laughter and to love and to have faith. I try each day to see God's will. I pray, "Oh Jesus, I surrender." . . . I console myself with the old Negro spiritual: "Sooner will be done the troubles of this world. I'm going home to live with God."

Living in God's presence made such joy possible, and thus Sister Thea gladdened the hearts of others with her gift of presence.

Creativity. People who have learned, through grace and hard work, to give life have the virtue of joy. In every classroom where real education is going on, the atmosphere is charged with joy, a creative, life-giving energy that challenges potential into fullness of being. Joyous creativity expands the heart and the soul.

Thérèse of Lisieux knew well the source of creative joy when she said: "Joy isn't found in the material objects surrounding us but in the inner recesses of the soul. One can possess joy in a prison cell as well as in a palace." This is possible, I would add, if joy has become a virtue in one's life. For if we are in a prison cell, cut off from family and friends, our soul might well sink into deep depression unless the creative power of joy—the expansive energy that readily seeks enlargement of life—draws us into the inner recesses of our soul where we have treasures that no one can take from us. Here the virtue of joy creates room for and delight in life even while surrounded by death.

Acceptance. I hold that joy, the basic disposition that enables us to see what Gerard Manley Hopkins called "the dearest freshness of deep down things," positions us to accept the ambiguity of human existence. Successes are embraced with gratitude. Failures become opportunities for growth. Everything becomes nourishment for one's own development as well as for the common good.

Julian of Norwich said, "And what can make us to rejoice more in God than to see in him that in us, of all his greatest works, he has joy?" Virtuously joyful persons live with the conviction that they are not only acceptable in God's sight, but are truly one of God's delights. Joy leads us to self-acceptance and the acceptance of others. More broadly, joy leads us to say yes to our existence.

Enthusiasm. Enthusiasm—energy incarnate—is a telltale sign that joy inflames the soul. Words are spoken with conviction, deeds are performed with confidence, thoughts are pursued with vigor and excitement. Other people tend to become infected by this healthy joy. The virtuous, joyful person is on the move, afire with warmth and light. As in all things, enthusiasm can be misguided, as witnessed in certain forms of fanaticism that disrespect basic human rights. But holy joy manifests itself through enthusiasm for what is life-giving.

Joy's Sibling, Suffering

Like many aspects of life, joy presents a paradox. Without its sibling, suffering, joy is almost impossible to comprehend. As Emily Dickinson wrote: "Success is counted sweetest / By those who ne'er succeed." More to the point, being human means that we suffer. Affliction becomes tolerable when we balance it with joy. The habit of the virtue of joy allows us to see through the suffering to the good.

The virtue of joy urges us to give our attention to the deep flow of God's amazing, reassuring, strengthening grace. Bertrand Weaver offers this analogy to explain the coexistence of joy and suffering:

> This famous current of warm water [the Gulf Stream], which flows from the Gulf of Mexico along the Eastern coast of North America, is separated from the coast by a narrow strip of cold water. The hardships of life may be compared with the cold-water strip that lies alongside the Gulf Stream. As the Gulf Stream proceeds on its way north, it tends to drag other water along with it. As more water becomes involved, its speed decreases and its boundaries become indefinite. In a similar way, the cold facts and events of life may prevent us from feeling sensibly the warmth of spiritual joy for long or short periods, but they cannot essentially affect that deep current of joy which is an effect of the presence of the Holy Spirit within us.

The Holy Spirit always offers the fruit of "love, joy, peace, patience, kindness, generosity, faithfulness, gentleness and self-control" (Galatians 5:22). We have only to dive into the flow of joy.

When Jesus told the disciples to become like little children, he was, in part, urging them to keep the childlike mind that always tries to see the good, even in the worst of circumstances. A good example of this comes from *The Diary of Anne Frank*. As a Jewish teenager, Anne Frank hid in an attic with her family to escape Nazi persecution. After they were discovered, Anne perished in a concentration camp. In the face of constant fear, she wrote:

> When I lie in bed and end my prayers with the words, "I thank you, God, for all that is good and dear and beautiful," I am filled with joy. Then I think about "the good" of going into hiding, of my health and with my whole being of the "dearness" of Peter . . . and of "the beauty" which exists in the world. . . .
>
> I don't think then of all the misery, but of the beauty that still remains. . . . Look at these things, then you find yourself again, and God, and then you regain your balance.

Even surrounded by fear, misery, and persecution, Anne leaned into life. Indeed, the beautiful, the good, the dear took on added pleasure because of the suffering all around her.

Suffering has a way of either thrusting us into the arms of God's loving embrace—true joy—or luring us into despair. To turn toward God in rejoicing brings us strength. As Psalm 46:4–7 declares:

> There is a river
> whose streams give joy to the city of God,
> the holy dwelling of the Most High.
> God is in its midst; it stands firm.

Suffering will always accompany joy. The grace of the virtue of joy—taking delight, gladdening hearts—makes suffering tolerable and even sharpens our gladness.

Growing Joy

A counselor, not known for her indirect methodology, responded to a client who said that she was burned out: "Honey, you can't be burned out; you were never on fire!" I am not too sure if this was a helpful comment, but it does speak about the importance of being on fire. To keep the fires of joy burning we need proper self-care. It seems to me that we grow joy—catch fire—by cultivating wonder, celebration, discipline, and good memory.

Wonder. The glory of God is everywhere, but unless we have a heart that wonders, we may miss it. To develop the virtue of joy, we thus need to nourish our sense of wonder or awe, seeing with our heart. Rabbi Abraham Joshua Heschel describes awe as "an intuition for the creaturely dignity of all things and their preciousness to God; a realization that things not only are what they are but also stand, however remotely, for something absolute. Awe is a sense for the transcendence." Heschel also offers a shorter description of wonder as "radical amazement."

Children stand in awe of life because every experience is new, fresh. To have the wonder and the joy of children requires that we open the eyes

14

of our heart through prayer, meditation, attention, play, and listening. Wonder can be cultivated in many small ways: by reminding ourselves that we are in God's sacred presence when we walk into a room, by asking more questions, by trying something new—becoming a beginner again, by being silent more often, by making our constant prayer these words of Isaiah,

"Holy, holy, holy is the [God] of hosts;
the whole earth is full of [God's] glory."
(6:3)

Celebration. The joyful person delights and takes pleasure in any sign of life. I once watched a grandfather as his grandchildren opened their Christmas gifts. As wrappings were torn open, smiles of delight from both the children and their grandfather outshone the shimmering lights on the evergreen. The delight, the joy took flesh as hugs were exchanged, thank-you's extended, songs of merriment and laughter erupted. The virtue of joy, the delighting, results in this celebrating, the enlarging of our soul, and the widening of our heart. Celebrating produces harmony and beauty, and so strengthens the virtue of joy.

All through the Bible, celebrating nourishes joy. The Psalms and other books of the Bible are filled with celebration. Psalm 47:1 proclaims: "All you peoples, clap your hands; / raise a joyful shout to God." Ephesians 5:18–19 states: "Be filled with the Spirit, as you sing psalms and hymns and spiritual songs among yourselves, singing and making melody to the Lord in your hearts."

A wonderful Jewish story nicely illustrates the way celebrating enlarges joy:

Rabbi Samuel bar Isaac regarded it as an act of virtue to rejoice with a bride and bridegroom. Whenever he came to a wedding he would take a twig of myrtle and dance gaily before the bride and groom.

Once Rabbi Ze'era saw him dance this way and felt ashamed of him.

"Just see how that old fool misbehaves!" he cried.

In time, Rabbi Samuel died. For three hours on end it thundered and lightning rent the heavens. In the midst of it a Celestial Voice cried out, "Woe! Woe! Rabbi Samuel bar Isaac is dead. Rise and pay him the last honors as he deserves!"

As the great throng followed him to his final resting place a column of fire descended from heaven. Miraculously, it was in the shape of a myrtle branch! It stood between the bier of the dead man and the mourners.

They all agreed that the great honor Heaven bestowed upon Rabbi Samuel was because of his efforts to gladden the hearts of the bride and the bridegroom by dancing before them with a twig of myrtle in his hand.

Celebrating springs from joy, but the roots of the virtue of joy are cultivated in celebrating. So dance, sing, send thank-you cards, and perform simple rituals for gifts given and deeds done.

Discipline. The virtue of joy also grows through discipline; that is, becoming a learner or pupil and thus a disciple. Joy is a seed that needs development, and development means taking the attitude of a learner. Discipline to nourish joy generally means attentively choosing to say yes to life. Christian discipline specifically means deliberately practicing meditation on God's loving word, reaching out to others in need, saying no to influences that throw us into depression. The adage, "No cows, no calcium!" could be paraphrased, "No discipline, no virtue!"

Good memory. Joy can be lost just like any precious coin. The virtue of faith is threatened by secularism and consumerism; hope is endangered by the reality of innocent suffering; charity is lost when narcissism creeps in and imprisons our soul in excessive self-preoccupation. Joy is lost when we forget that we are surrounded by God's extravagant blessing and when we fail to exercise this virtue as occasions arise. Forgetting is especially dangerous for it causes disorientation and a cutting off from our center. The branch is joyous as long as it is attached to the vine with a certain level of consciousness and apprehension. As soon as it forgets, the withering begins.

Praying for Joy

I'm convinced that what we are close to gets inside us, be that cigar smoke or Chanel No. 5, the wisdom of Plato or the integrity of Saint

Thomas More, the beauty of classical music or the chaos of decadent art. We are susceptible to influences in ways we cannot even imagine. We are susceptible to joy.

This book "exposes" us to thirty-one reflections on joy with a commentary and some questions. To spend quality time with joyful people and their writings might well transform our heart and soul. As you pray each day, practice joy. Let the passages and reflections invite you to rejoice and delight. Remember Rabbi Samuel who was blessed by God for dancing. Remember the Ephesians singing songs.

Johnny Appleseed was a man of hope as he spread apple seeds across the land. I hope that you who prays these pages may find the seed of joy germinating in your soul and producing a rich harvest—a harvest that will last.

31

Reflections

on Joy

1.

Juice and Joy

Listen

Nothing is so beautiful as spring—
>   When weeds, in wheels, shoot long and
>   lovely and lush;
>   Thrush's eggs look little low heavens,
>   and thrush
Through the echoing timber does so rinse
>   and wring
The ear, it strikes like lightnings to hear him sing;
>   The glassy peartree leaves and blooms, they
>   brush
>   The descending blue; that blue is all in a rush
With richness; the racing lambs too have fair
>   their fling.

What is all this juice and all this joy?
>   A strain of the earth's sweet being in
>   the beginning
In Eden garden. —Have, get, before it cloy,
>   Before it cloud, Christ, lord, and sour
>   with sinning,
Innocent mind and Mayday in girl and boy,
>   Most, O maid's child, thy choice and worthy
>   the winning.

(Gerard Manley Hopkins)

Reflect

Spring is a juicy season. The sap runs in the maple trees, snow turns into water and rushes to the creek, and even human blood quickens. All this movement, inner and outer, speaks of new life. This juice is a joy. Beauty and joy commingle at the intersection of spring. Nature longs to find expression for this inner spirit of delight and pleasure. Joy is beauty's song.

This is not to say that there is no joy in winter when the ice crystals on the window pane delight the soul. Or that autumn is joyless, for who cannot laugh and sing when the leaves turn golden? Or that summer is not without its delights, the harvest creeping toward fulfillment. Spring has no monopoly on joy. But spring does claim that vernal joy cannot be outdone by any other season. The juice is evidence for this; an expanded heart confirms the conviction.

What joys do you find in springtime? Name the joys of the other seasons of your life. How juicy are your joys?

Respond

God of all seasons, and God of all joys, help us to be present to your divine love, the source of all true delight. Your gift of new life, spring or winter, summer or fall, is the cause of our joy and the root of our peace.

Help us to be a people filled with springtime and always willing to bear your life to others.

2.

A Quivering Needle

Listen

Yet [Christian] joy is as mysterious and as un-fathomable as the character of sanctity itself, and like sanctity and holiness it seems never to have been the goal, but only the by-product of the soul's attachment to God.

Joy is such an utterly different category from pleasure or the absence of pain. It is a quivering needle between the soul's utter satisfaction and its contrary sense of its own bent toward nothing-ness, between what Simone Weil so subtly calls Grace and its natural countering downthrust *Gravity*. To "weep for joy" is ever so natural because joy lies both between and beyond both tears and laughter. Yet there is a great lightening of the heart in it and a healing that knows no equal. To a heart that has known its balm, there can be the merriness of the scaffold itself of a Thomas More who asks the Lord Lieutenant to help him up the ladder with a genial "and as for my coming down, let me shift for myself."

(Douglas V. Steere)

Reflect

I've seen joy in dogs as their whole body quivers at the sight of their master's return. The tail wags, the ears perk up when the voice is heard. I've seen it, this joy, in airports and bus stations when friends once again come together. It's in the words, the glances, the hugs. All is aquiver with unfathomable presence.

This joy embraces tears and laughter, but it is not held by them. This quivering joy transcends the lexicon of pleasure and pain, dwelling near the border of ecstasy, and thus, eternity. For all its lightness it is a grave grace, a by-product of love that conquers death.

Name the places where you have quivered with joy. What does joy do to your heart? Have joy and holiness been connected for you?

Respond

God of joy and peace,
>your love is beyond all pleasure and pain,
>your grace beyond all tears and laughter.
In our oneness with you, we quiver with joy,
>when apart from you,
>we are stilled with sadness.
Your Spirit of joy lightens and heals our heart.
For all this, we give you thanks and praise.

3.

Surprised by Joy

Listen

The most important experiences of [C. S. Lewis's] childhood, indeed, of his whole life, were not literary. They were mystical experiences of the presence of God. . . . They arose from seemingly incongruous events, incongruous, that is, until one remembers that the spirit blows where it listeth. He chose the word "joy" to describe these experiences. It is the best possible word, the shortest and fullest. Joy is the ever-present, central quality in all forms of religious experience. The first time it came to him from the memory of a small garden that his brother had made for him out of a biscuit tin filled with moss, stones, twigs, and tiny flowers. It came again while he was reading a book by Beatrix Potter, his favorite, *Squirrel Nutkin*. He valued these experiences of joy more than anything else he had known, and he desired, as all who have experienced them desire, to have them again and again. It was this mystical quality that set him apart from other boys. He was surprised by joy. He spent the rest of his life searching for more of it.

(George Sayer)

Reflect

Joy takes us by surprise because it is the gift and experience of the presence of God. Sometimes it comes in remembering a brother's present, sometimes in reading a book about animals, sometimes in meeting one's beloved. God's presence is mediated in thousands of ways.

Once one has tasted joy, the search is on for more. There is a danger here, the quest can be so intensive that one's capacity to be surprised might be diminished. But for all that, one's ear is always attuned for more. Joy invokes communion, which is an aspect of mysticism. Joy is oneness with God and that immediacy makes the mystic a person of joy.

When was the last time you were surprised by joy? What books have caused you joy? Why? What memories lead you to the door of joy?

Respond

God of surprises, help us to see
    that we are surrounded by miracles of joy.
Drive away our sadness and despair.
Empower us to be vulnerable to your nearness,
    the source of all joy,
    the source of all peace.

4.

A Net of Love

Listen

Joy is prayer—joy is strength—joy is love—joy is a net of love by which you can catch souls. God loves a cheerful giver. She gives most who gives with joy. The best way to show our gratitude to God and the people is to accept everything with joy, A joyful heart is the inevitable result of a heart burning with love. Never let anything so fill you with sorrow as to make you forget the joy of the Christ risen.

(Mother Teresa of Calcutta)

Reflect

When our heart is burning with love we experience joy. This joy becomes a net that enfolds others with its happy contagion. The fire spreads, the net expands, a new heaven and a new earth are under way.

A primary rule of Christian discipleship is to give and accept all with joy. By so doing we express an authentic gratitude while giving God honor and glory. This demands strength, courage, prayer, and faith. Most of all it demands love, which is the wellspring of joy.

Sorrow will come, often in great numbers. Grief will tear our soul apart. Loss may throw us into darkness. Yet the Risen Christ is for us and with us. To remember his presence once again re-establishes joy in our heart.

Ponder instances when you were a cheerful giver, a joyful recipient. When does your heart burn with love? Sing a favorite hymn to the Risen Christ.

Respond

Jesus, our risen savior,
    draw near to us who bear heavy burdens.
Fill our heart with the fire of your love,
    gift us with joy and make us truly grateful.
May all that we do and endure
    be done in and through your Spirit of joy.

5.

Everlasting Elements

Listen

My joys here are great, because they are very simple and spring from the everlasting elements: the pure air, the sun, the sea and the wheaten loaf.

(Nikos Kazantzakis)

Reflect

Great joys are found in simple things: a balloon rising in the pure air, a hawk circling in the evening sun, a wave tossing a swimmer to and fro, a breaking of bread with a friend. These are simple things available to any sensitive soul. These are great joys for the pure of heart.

We need again to return to the elements of air, water, sun, and earth. The early Greek philosophers honored these mysteries and used them to explain reality. Joy lies in homecoming; coming back to the fundamental ingredients of our being. Unless we foolishly resist, we are drawn like a magnet to taste the bread of life, to embrace the sunbeams, to be gifted by the sea, to ride the winds of life. Herein is much delight. Especially in times of illness and despondency, we are well advised to draw near to these everlasting elements. Nature is curative when we enter its domain as a partner. The light, be it physical, psychological, or spiritual, confronts our darkness and attempts to illumine the truth.

If you can, go out into the air and sun. Breathe deeply. Luxuriate in the sun on your skin. Slowly eat a slice of your favorite bread. If you cannot go out, or if eating is inconvenient, use your memory to recollect air, sun, sea, and bread. Ponder other simple delights and how they have helped you come to healing.

Respond

God of wind and sea,
    creator of sun and earth,
    fill us with the joy of your creation.
May we come to experience the simple things
    of life in great ways.
Grant us the wisdom to return again
    to the works of your hands
    and to come away refreshed and renewed.
Then we witness to the joy of your Reign,
    for ever and ever.

6.

The Pleasure of Service

Listen

Such service can have no meaning unless one takes pleasure in it. When it is done for show or for fear of public opinion, it stunts the man and crushes his spirit. Service which is rendered without joy helps neither the servant nor the served. But all other pleasures and possessions pale into nothingness before service which is rendered in a spirit of joy.

(Mohandas K. Gandhi)

Reflect

A dour-looking host is a dreaded thing. Called to be gracious and to take pleasure in the presence of guests, the reluctant host poisons the atmosphere by being unwilling to offer joyful service. Everyone hopes that the event will quickly end.

But experience willing, joyful hospitality, and all is made new. People feel their dignity, know affection, and realize the mystery of love. Even the most difficult duties, when rendered in a spirit of joy, become a light yoke, an easy burden. This is possible because the joy is grounded in a realistic love.

George Herbert wisely wrote: "All worldly joys go less / To the one joy of doing kindnesses." Reflect on how you give service. Is joy there? Have you ever felt the chill of joyless service? Give thanks for three joyful servants who have crossed your path.

Respond

Gracious Jesus,
    you came to serve,
    not to be served.
All you did flowed from love
    and was filled with joy.
Give us, we pray, your Spirit of joy,
    that we may do deeds of kindness
    with delight and fervor.
Grant this in your name.

7.

The Very Color of Holiness

Listen

As his life drew toward its close, Paul seems to have felt more and more the holy character of joy. Philippians, his last epistle, is full of joy. It drenches every line of that glorious little letter, written from prison in the shadow of death. And ever since Paul's day, joy, which is the very color of holiness, has been the one quality which the Church has always demanded and gotten from her saints. This is inevitable, for it is the mark of perfect consecration, the mysterious result of that complete surrender and death of self which is sanctity. Joy is not a luxury, it is a duty of the soul.

(Evelyn Underhill)

Reflect

Holiness has a number of markings: simplicity, poverty, obedience, and, of course, joy. Since holiness is the perfection of love, we need not be surprised to be instructed that joy gives evidence of sanctity. As love effects joy, joy in turn stirs the heart to song.

Our ordinary understanding of joy seems to exclude illness, persecution, disappointment, and failure. Yet Saint Paul, having experienced all kinds of difficulties, maintained joy. These graces flowed from his consecration to the person of Christ and from Christ's commitment to abide with Paul. Joy comes from presence.

Joy is a gift and a duty. God's power and grace make us capable of putting the interests and welfare of others above self-interest. When sensitive to being deeply gifted, we then can fulfill our obligations with joyful asceticism.

Consider a recent time of suffering, doubt, or conflict. Did you seek to rejoice in the good alongside the bad? Converse with Jesus about bringing joy to this pain.

Respond

God, our divine artist,
> color our days with holiness,
> the perfection of charity.
Then we will be a joyful people,
> and we will look redeemed.
Do not let us live drab existences,
> but rather be filled with enthusiasm
> and exuberant about life.

8.

Let My Soul in Song Declare

Listen

Land that was desolate, impassable,
is forest now where secrets find their voices.
The desert is inhabited and blooms.
One with the meadow, wilderness rejoices.

Lebanon's glory is its green possession
and Carmel's beauty. Visited by love,
wastelands are pastures for the Lamb at midday,
And living solitudes to hold the Dove.

Never again will patriarch prefigure
or lean precursor walk or prophet call.
Here is fulfillment. One has come and given
the Spirit Who is flame and festival.

Sower and Sown are here. The bright
     groves flourish
and burn toward islands in the utmost sea.
Time has become a wilderness of presence
which too is essence of its jubilee.

Earth keeps its seasons and its liturgy,
as should the soul. Oh, come, green summer, blur

these wastes and let my soul in song declare
Who came by flesh and Who by fire to her.

(Jessica Powers)

Reflect

When desolate land blooms, when wastelands are visited by rain, when the Spirit comes to those in solitude, joy breaks upon the land and soul. Secrets find their voice, and the festival gets under way.

On our earthly sojourn, waiting is long and the darkness can be terrifying. But when God's spirit inflames our soul with love, then the wilderness and our soul rejoice. Invite the summer into your soul now. Imagine the warmth and light of the Holy Spirit glowing in your soul. Sing the hymn, "How Can I Keep from Singing."

Respond

God of flame and festival,
     bring your Reign to fulfillment in us.
Visit us with your love,
     and we shall sing your glory and peace.

9.

The Road to Joy

Listen

On 13 May 1967, Thomas Merton wrote to
Grace Sisson, the daughter of one of his many
friends, thanking her for the drawing she had
sent called *The Road to Joy*.

I want especially to thank you for your note
and for your new drawing which is very signifi-
cant.

I like the way you see all the little creatures
tending toward a tree which is a sort of tree of
life. I am glad you still draw things with love,
and I hope you will never lose that. But I hope
you and I together will secretly travel our own
road to joy, which is mysteriously revealed to
us without our exactly realizing. When I say
that, I don't want you to start thinking about
it. You already know it without thinking
about it.

Well, you must be getting to be a big girl by
now. Your handwriting is that of a mature
little person and is in fact better than mine. I
hope you will write to me again. Say hello to
your Dad [Elbert R. Sisson] and to all the
family.

(Thomas Merton)

Reflect

Joy comes from the presence of companions on the journey. Partial joy is experienced through the gift of friendship, full joy when we travel with God too. The road to joy is peopled and divinized.

Other roads can be chosen, other destinies sought. The precious gift of freedom enables us to decide what path and companions will be ours. One can choose death, not life; sadness, not joy. Such a choice makes all the difference in the world and beyond.

Merton drew many joyful images. Draw or paint your road to joy. Even if you are not skilled in art, assume a childlike mind and let go. Sketch in your companions on the road and other delights and ways you bring gladness to life.

Respond

Faithful God,
    reveal to us today the road to joy.
When we are lost and anxious
    about almost everything,
    you come to guide us home.
Be our daily companion.
Then we will know, by your presence,
    the joy that comes from love.
Grant this through Jesus, who is the Way.

10.

Be Glad

Listen

Dear friends, as you always obeyed me when I was with you, it is even more important that you obey me now while I am away from you. Keep on working with fear and trembling to complete your salvation, because God is always at work in you to make you willing and able to obey [God's] own purpose.

Do everything without complaining or arguing, so that you may be innocent and pure as God's perfect children, who live in a world of corrupt and sinful people. You must shine among them like stars lighting up the sky, as you offer them the message of life. If you do so, I shall have reason to be proud of you on the Day of Christ, because it will show that all my effort and work have not been wasted.

Perhaps my life's blood is to be poured out like an offering on the sacrifice that your faith offers to God. If that is so, I am glad and share my joy with you all. In the same way, you too must be glad and share your joy with me.

(Philippians 2:12-18)

Reflect

Joy flows out of faith. Only deep faith in the things of God enables a person to speak in one and the same breath about shedding one's blood and rejoicing in such an offering. Saint Paul does exactly that in his Letter to the Philippians. He speaks about being glad and joyful in doing God's will, even though that means suffering and death.

At the same time Paul offers his joy and desires to be the recipient of the joy in the heart of his people. Joy needs to be given. Like Paul and the Philippians, we are to shine like stars in the night sky. Herein is cause for rejoicing. The darkness cannot conquer the light of joy. Sadness gives way to gladness because the day of the Redeemer is near, is now.

Recall a time when joy and sacrifice went hand in hand, and when you realized that joy had to be mutual. Have you celebrated mutual joy recently? Isn't it time to do so?

Respond

God of our salvation,
    you are always working in our world,
    in our soul.
Transform our darkness to light,
    our sorrow to joy.
Empower us to find our joy in you and your will
    and to share our joy with all whom we meet.
Let us go rejoicing.

11.

Terrible Joy

Listen

Marvelous Truth, confront us
at every turn,
in every guise, iron ball,
egg, dark horse, shadow,
cloud
of breath on the air,

dwell
in our crowded hearts
our steaming bathrooms, kitchens full of
things to be done, the
ordinary streets.

Thrust close your smile
that we know you, terrible joy.

(Denise Levertov)

Reflect

Joy can be terrible; that is, it can be so over-
whelming that it causes terror in the soul. One
need but think of the account of Christ's

Resurrection in which the disciples experience fright and abundant joy in the same encounter. Joy is terrible because it stems from marvelous truth. When confronted time and again by beauty, when visited day after day by grace, when smiled upon by love, what else can the soul do but rejoice?

Terrible joy born of marvelous truth is ubiquitous. It can be met in a shadow, discovered in our crowded streets and crowded hearts, known in the radiance of a mystical countenance. For those who know the truth by faith, joy is present everywhere. It is a terrible grace, but it does not leave us terrified.

Recall some terrible joys in your experience. How does God "confront" you, "dwell," or "thrust close" in your life?

Respond

God of truth and joy,
    we praise and thank you for your glory.
In every place and at every moment
    you are near to us,
    showering us with grace and love.
Guide us always by your truth,
    fill us always with your joy,
    that we might witness to you in our world.

12.

Even Nailed to a Tree

Listen

Joy is where the whole being is pointed in one direction, and it is something that by its nature a man never hoards but always wants to share. The second thing is that joy is a mystery because it can happen anywhere, anytime, even under the most unpromising circumstances, even in the midst of suffering, with tears in its eyes. Even nailed to a tree.

What Jesus is saying is that men are made for joy and that anyone who is truly joyous has a right to say that he is doing God's will on this earth. Where you have known joy, you have known him. We are the monkey-gods, of course—monkeys in origin, the sons of God in destiny, outrageous and ludicrous, vain and boastful. And in answer to all our words about ourselves, about the meaning of life, about him, the God who made us holds up before our wondering eyes not just [a] hand, like the Buddha, but the figure of a man whose face is marred almost beyond human semblance but who says, "These things I have spoken to you, have done for you, have died for you, that my joy may be in you, and that your joy may be made full."

(Frederick Buechner)

42

Reflect

Joy is focused, overflowing, mysterious, and ubiquitous. That it can be found anywhere and at anytime brings hope to the human heart. Even in moments of crucifixion, joy is at work as is its accomplice, peace. We are made for joy. When the Spirit is upon us, we are probably in the right place doing the right work. Joy gives a certitude that no epistemology can fathom.

Slowly and meditatively repeat the words, "We are made for joy," over and over, letting them seep into your heart. Then pronounce these words as you consider places of personal pain.

Respond

Gracious and joyous God,
    we struggle to know and do your will.
Send us joy in our service to others.
Help us to see that by dying to our selfishness
    we are free to follow the mission of Jesus,
        the Lord of joy and Prince of Peace.
Come, Spirit of joy, come.

13.

Joyful Wine

Listen

What can we understand by the joy of wine?
There is still more joy here; not only the joy of
survival, but the joy of celebration, of friendship,
of the banquet, of the nuptials, of love, of new
life, of victory.

The joy of wine is a sign of enthusiasm, of
simplicity, of interior quiet; it is a symbol of the
loosening of inhibitions, of fears which impede
reciprocal communication. In the Bible, just as in
the history of culture, wine is the symbol of a life
which is unfolding, freely expanding, defining
itself.

In the opposite sense, the lack of wine, in
cultural and biblical symbolism, always means
closing down, stiffening, creating suspicion, sadness, irritability, touchiness, argumentativeness,
bad temper, pessimism, corrosive criticism,
sourness.

(Cardinal Carlo Maria Martini)

Reflect

We seek symbols for the major themes in our life.
Love finds expression in a ring; reconciliation in

the shaking of hands; joy in the taste of wine. Fermented grapes have a power to expand our life and foster dialog. In excess, wine can kill the spirit and the body. A glass of wine shared between friends is a sacred moment. When listening is deep and the truth is spoken, the bonding that happens might well be labeled joy. And it is difficult to locate this bonding's exact source: a word, a glance, a breath, a smile.

Too much of life is joyless, infected by sadness, suspicion, and sourness. Complicity replaces simplicity, and we get lost. Shutting down replaces enthusiasm, and we are paralyzed. Criticism snows under our small affirmations, and we no longer celebrate. We must return to Cana time and again and taste the water made into wine.

Do a calm but thorough examination of any joyless part of your personality. How can you replace it with rejoicing, delighting, and taking pleasure—joyful wine?

Respond

Spirit of peace and joy,
    fill us with the graced wine of your love.
Help us to bring joy to others,
    especially those in deep and constant pain.
Replace our sadness and sourness with
            celebration
        that we might manifest your presence to
            others.

14.

On with the Dance

Listen

Did ye not hear it?—No; 'twas but the wind,
    Or the car rattling o'er the stony street;
    On with the dance! let joy be unconfined;
    No sleep till morn, when Youth and Pleasure
        meet
    To chase the glowing Hours with flying feet.
                 (Lord Byron)

Reflect

Dance is intriguing. The body and soul merge in a spontaneity so powerful that even the observer is pushed toward the edge of ecstasy. Dance is unconfined in its paradoxically disciplined rhythm. Music and dancers commingle in a dynamic intimacy that speaks both of life and death.

Joy is intriguing. It too must be unconfined like the rapture of a child caught in happy surprise. The moment constraints are imposed, the joy ceases. The inner dance ends, though movement is still seen on the dance floor.

There is a season for everything—in the loss of a beloved, unconfined sorrow; in the presence of those we love, unconfined joy. Most of life carries constraints. So be it. But there are days (even seasons) when we leave our confinement and taste the wind of bliss.

Play with good memories of times when your soul danced. Indeed, if you can, put on some music or hum to yourself and dance. If anything constrains you, acknowledge it and then wish it good-bye.

Respond

Unconfined God,
    lover of dance and liberty,
    plunge us deep into the heart of mystery.
Remove the shackles of ignorance and fear.
Free us to live in your Spirit
of enthusiasm and joy.
Teach us the dance of grace,
    and we will give full glory and praise.

15.

Christian Optimism

Listen

The Gospel, above all else, is *the joy of creation*. God, who in creating saw . . . creation was good (cf. Genesis 1:1–25), is the source of joy for all creatures, and above all for humankind. God the Creator seems to say of all creation: "It is good that you exist." And [God's] joy spreads especially through the "good news," according to which *good is greater than all that is evil in the world*. Evil, in fact, is neither fundamental nor definitive. This point clearly distinguishes Christianity from all forms of existential pessimism.

(John Paul II)

Reflect

In the Book of Genesis, God keeps pronouncing that creation is good, very good. We are part of that creation. It is good that we exist. The psalmist reminds us that God takes delight in the divine creation. Good News indeed. Herein we discover a source of joy.

Because of evil in the world, there is a danger of buying into an existential pessimism. A brief glance at history and its atrocities can overwhelm the human spirit and endanger the experience of joy. Faith, however, draws us back into reality. Good is greater than evil. God's joy spreads down through the ages enabling us to witness to the Good News of salvation. Joy is fundamental and definitive.

Look around you at creation. Pronounce the creator's words on what you see, feel, taste, smell, and hear: "It is good, very good." Recall the many evils around you, ask God to see through them to the good.

Respond

God, our creator,
　　you have made all things well
　　and fill creation with grandeur and joy.
When evil comes,
　　do not let us despair,
　　but rather put our hope in you.
Make us instruments of joy.
May we thank you always for your goodness.

16.

Anticipation of Excitement

Listen

I no longer believe we can slug out a lifetime of Christian witness by placing our total offering on an altar marked "obligation." There has got to be a measure of *joy* in what we do, an anticipation of excitement when we face the day, rather than a dull feeling of boredom or resentment at what lies ahead. Some may call this "selfish" (Calvinists immediately begin to cover their tracks), but I am surer and surer that unless there *is* joy in what we do, the results will not only be drab and cheerless for us but also for those with whom we work.

(Robert McAfee Brown)

Reflect

There is something admirable in people who faithfully embrace their duties and obligations even though what has to be done carries with it no personal reward or periodic delight: visiting an Alzheimer's patient week after week, month after month in a nursing home, doing the weekly laundry for the zillionth time, revisiting past wounds in an attempt to integrate them into one's life. But our responsibilities need a measure of joy. We need the energy of enthusiasm even in the most menial tasks if we are to avoid resentment and boredom, if we are to bring life to ourselves and others. A joyless, drab existence is a sorry sight. Worse, it is a wasted life.

Two graces are needed here: wisdom to help us see wherein joy lies, and courage to transcend the downward pull of duty's gravity. Joy cannot be self-induced. It arises out of a loving presence that supports and sustains us. We thus offer at the altar the gift of joy planted earlier in our heart.

What obligations or duties do you find boring and tempt you to harbor resentment? Set your creativity to work, asking the Holy Spirit to help you bring joy to these tasks.

Respond

God of life and freedom,
> you call us to be responsible pilgrims,
> conscious of our duties
> and committed to the common good.
Guide us in your way.
Enkindle in us the fire of joy
> so that whatever we do may give you glory
> and lead all of us and others to fullness
> of life.

17.

Joy Has No Smugness

Listen

Something shone from that man [Louis Armstrong], a rare thing, real *joy*. It is becoming exceedingly rare among artists of any kind. And I have an idea that those who can and do communicate it are always people who have had a hard time. Then the joy has no smugness or self-righteousness in it, is inclusive not exclusive, and comes close to prayer.

(May Sarton)

Reflect

The creativity of artists, in its life-giving thrust, would certainly seem to lead to joy. However, two dispositions wall out joy: the smugness arising from a sense of arrogant superiority and a distasteful self-righteousness that makes some creative people repugnant. Joy finds no lodging in the house of exclusivity.

Somehow prayer and joy share the same family of origin. The artists who radiate joy have been humbled by trials, every strain of smugness broken. These artists also live with an awareness that their gift is precisely that—a gift—and that fact shatters self-righteousness. Little is left but prayers of thanksgiving and intercessions for help in time of need. Herein lies an inclusive joy that is exceedingly rare and beautiful.

Pose this hard question to yourself: Do I suffer from smugness or self-righteousness? Try to get in touch with occasions that trigger these behaviors. Pray over these times, and ask how to bring joy in these circumstances.

Respond

Divine Artist, God our creator,
    instruct us in the ways of joy.
All too often we turn away from you
    toward narrow self-reliance.
Too soon we seek our own path that leads
    away from you.
Send your Spirit of joy, humility, and truth
    into our heart.
Then we will recognize you,
    not only in the breaking of bread and word,
    but also in the exceedingly abundant grace
      of your love,
    our joy.

18.

A Reward of Creation

Listen

It has been said that joy is the reward of creation, the sign that we are spiritually alive and at work, and no doubt it is true that unless we do have joy in our work, we shall never do anything really well. But I think that Christian joy goes far deeper than this. It is a grace that comes from God, a grace that irradiates us when we cease to resist in any way [God's] action upon our souls.

(Evelyn Underhill)

Reflect

Saint Paul lists joy as one of the signs of the Holy Spirit in our life. To be alive spiritually therefore implies the presence of joy. A cursory glance verifies this observation. People who are deeply alive radiate joy.

To perform work well and for it to have a lasting effect, joy is a major ingredient. One might argue that a grumpy heart surgeon may be successful in his or her craft even though there isn't an ounce of joy in his or her body. But experience and even research shows that physical healing occurs more rapidly when glad energy surrounds a patient. Joylessness diminishes the possibility of full health of soul, mind, and heart.

Going a step deeper: Christian joy is a gift from God that we call grace. We need but yield to the sunbeams of this blessing to fill our soul and heart. When joy is readily embraced and shared, the glory of God is upon the land. Creation's reward is joy for all those who abide in God's creative love.

Ponder the way you go about your work: Do you bring delight and gladness to it? How can you open yourself more to the grace of joy in your work?

Respond

God of creation and of joy,
  you long to share your blessings with us.
Send the Spirit of joy into our heart
  that our work and leisure
  may be done in delight,
  and that our worship and love
  may be filled with your peace.
Lead us gently into your abundant love.

19.

Led into Joy

Listen

If relatedness rather than aloneness is our fundamental reality and not just a hopelessly longed-
for state, then recognition or fulfillment of that
relatedness might well induce joy.

(Nel Noddings)

Reflect

Is our fundamental reality relatedness or aloneness? The answer to this question conditions the
whole of one's personal existence as well as larger
social issues. Is rugged individualism or interde-
pendence the salient feature of our humanness?
The possibility of joy hangs in the balance.

If our identity consists of being fiercely inde-
pendent nomads, nothing will be able to induce a
sustained joy. If, however, we are social by nature
and find fulfillment in sharing and intimacy,
then joy may become a way of life.

What technology will lead us to the fulfillment
of relatedness? Perhaps only the technology of
love. The "computer chips" here are concern and
respect, reverence and thoughtfulness.

What sort of balance do you have between relatedness and aloneness in your life? Ponder the joy of relatedness and how you have induced joy by reaching out to other people.

Respond

Mysterious God,
>   your life reminds us
>   that relationships are at the heart of reality.
Deepen our experiences of your presence
>   in our life.
Save us from a false isolation
>   that inhibits all peace and joy.
Bring us back again into the light of your love,
>   for herein we find life and graced joy.

20.

The Sweetness of Contact

Listen

We know then that joy is the sweetness of contact with the love of God, that affliction is the wound of this same contact when it is painful, and that only the contact matters, not the manner of it.

(Simone Weil)

Reflect

Drawing near to God is at the heart of the spiritual journey. Making contact can result in either joy or affliction: joy when the contact is filled with delight, affliction when we encounter God with suffering. Priority must be given to the contact, and not to the joy or affliction.

Several images convey aspects of joy's sweetness: song, laughter, sunshine. By contrast, affliction is in the room when somber silence, tears, and darkness descend. Weil reminds us that what matters is that God is here with us now! Happiness is grounded in presence, not in the emotional consequences of sweet or painful contact.

To make the paradox complete we speak of and can experience tears of joy. Amid the severest

loss that produces copious tears, we can still experience God's abiding love that causes our heart to
exalt in quiet secrecy.

What has been your experience of tears of joy?
Have you ever felt afflicted when you drew near
to God? Talk to God about this paradox.

Respond

God of joy and affliction, of laughter and tears,
    of ecstasy and anguish,
      may we forget ourselves and abandon
      ourselves to your will.
When you are near, we feel peace and joy.
Do not allow us to drift away from your love,
    the source of our joy.
Send your Spirit to keep us faithful to your way.

21.

In Harmony

Listen

For it was a spiritual joy; my soul knew that here was a soul that would understand and be in harmony with mine.

(Teresa of Ávila)

Reflect

We experience joy in many ways: physical joy —taking delight in an ice cream sundae; psychological joy—accepting a word of affirmation; and so on. And then there is the joy of one soul in tune with another, the joy of affinity, a spiritual joy. Another name for this joy is friendship. Two people share the same vision, a common understanding, an intrinsic harmony that mysteriously bonds their souls. Having come together in a gracious commingling, it is difficult to identify where one soul ends and the other begins. Boundaries have been transcended by mutual affection.

Such a spiritual joy cannot be planned, but we can open our soul to it. Then in this bonding of true friendship, two individuals share their hopes and fears, strengths and weaknesses, and experience a spiritual joy; the joy of union. Like the sudden surprise of a rainbow, the individual colors unite into the beauty of this miracle.

Close your eyes and see your friends, those soul mates in whom you rejoice. Offer words of thanks and rejoicing to your Divine Friend, the source of all friendship and joy.

Respond

Spirit of the living God,
> guide us in the way of understanding
> and unity.
Help us open our soul to spiritual joys,
> the joy of friendship with others
> and with you.
We long to live in harmony with your will,
> for herein is the source and summit of all joy.
Send your Spirit to empower us,
> for your will is sacred friendship.

22.

Quicken My Spirit

Listen

O everlasting Light, far surpassing all created things, send down the beams of Your brightness from above, and purify, gladden, and illuminate in me all the inward corners of my heart. Quicken my spirit with all its powers, that it may cleave fast and be joined to You in joyful gladness of spiritual rapture. Oh, when will that blessed hour come when You will visit me and gladden me with Your blessed presence, so that You are to me all in all. As long as that gift is not given me, there will be in me no full joy.

(Thomas à Kempis)

Reflect

Mark Twain knew well the power of lightning and the choice of the right word. "The difference between the right word and the nearly right word is the difference between lightning and a lightning bug." God's light is lightning—bright and alive, cleansing and transforming. When that light, with all its power and glory, pierces our inmost heart we are made glad because it drives out all darkness and coldness. Saint Paul was once hit by lightning, and it killed his old self. The right Word, Jesus the Lord, made clear and glad and bright and alive the inmost part of his heart. Paul's theme song would forever be ecstatic joy, "Rejoice in the Lord always; again I will say, Rejoice" (Philippians 4:4).

Joy is a gift, an expansive and expensive grace. But to be in a position to embrace this blessing we must place ourselves in the path of lightning. Remaining in our comfort zones of sensuality, hiding behind the armor of false pride, refusing to accept the tempest of messy ministry are all evasive tactics that block the possibility of the ecstasy of joy.

When, where, and how do you expose yourself to God's lightning? at church? at the kitchen table? in your garden? at work? Remember encounters with God's light and say with Paul, "Again I will say, Rejoice."

Respond

God of light and lightning,
>   illumine our world and our heart
>   with your love.
We are poor, small, narrow creatures,
>   often devoid of joy and weary with waiting.
Flash forth your truth and your love,
>   and we shall witness to your glory.
Expand our heart with joyful light this day.

23.

God Joys in Us

Listen

And the greatest light and the brightest shining . . . is the glorious love of our Lord God, as I see it. And what can make us to rejoice more in God than to see in him that in us, of all his greatest works, he has joy? . . . [The Trinity] made man's soul as beautiful, as good, as precious a creature as it could make. . . . And it wants our hearts to be powerfully lifted above the depths of the earth and all empty sorrows, and to rejoice in it.

(Julian of Norwich)

Reflect

William Blake's poem "The Tiger" magnificently describes the fierce feature of the tiger. Suddenly the poet startles us by raising the question of God's joy. "Did he smile his work [the tiger] to see, / Did he who made the lamb make thee?" Of course the answer is yes. God rejoices in creation, but the Incarnation shows us that God delights most in finite, fragile, bumbling human beings.

The reverse is also true. God's deepest sadness lies in failed humanity. Jesus weeps over Jerusalem. Saint Paul tells us not to grieve the Holy Spirit through sin. We are created to lift powerfully our heart in rejoicing.

Ponder the last couple of days, and consider what you have done that would make God smile. In what way are you a channel of God's joy? What response arises in your heart when you are the object of joy?

Respond

God of all creation,
>   you who made the tiger and the lamb,
>   the moon and the stars and all humankind,
>   smile upon us with love and mercy.
Reveal to us the joy of your heart,
>   and give us joy to delight in you
>   and all your work.
Place a song of thanksgiving and peace
>   in our heart.

24.

Deepest Inducement

Listen

Slowly learning this: to live, to have patience, to work, and never to miss an inducement to joy. For this wise and great man [Rodin] knows how to find joy, friend; a joy as nameless as that one remembers from childhood, and yet full to the brim with the deepest inducement; the smallest things come to him and open up to him; a chestnut that we find, a stone, a shell in the gravel, everything speaks as though it had been in the wilderness and had meditated and fasted. And we have almost nothing to do but listen; for work itself comes out of this listening; one must lift it out with both arms, for it is heavy.

(Rainer Maria Rilke)

Reflect

Waiting and listening are difficult arts. They require the ability to stay with emptiness and treat it as a friend. But the consequence is worth every ounce of patience—the consequence is joy. The Latin proverb *Ubi patientia, ibi laetitia*— where there is patience, there is joy—is accurate.

Not to miss a single inducement (from *inducere*, to lead on) to joy is a high degree of maturity. Nameless joys come in the smallest things: chest-nuts, pebbles, shells, acorns, peas, gnats, butter-flies. Quiet attentiveness brings an unfolding and an intimacy filled with delight. No strenuous effort is necessary. Rather, all that is needed is a reverent listening of the heart and soul.

Inducing birth leads to pain, but compare the suffering to the joy when the mother takes her baby into her arms. In the joy of new life, pain is forgotten. When has patience and listening led you to opening up to unfolding joy? Listen now. . .

Respond

Divine physician, induce your life with us,
  a life of love, joy, and peace.
Teach us how to listen to your creation,
  the atom, the stars, the bumblebee.
Keep us present to the mystery of your love,
  and we will know again your terrible joy.

25.

Crimson Joy

Listen

O Rose, thou art sick!
    The invisible worm
    That flies in the night,
    In the howling storm,

    Hast found out thy bed
    Of crimson joy,
    And his dark secret love
    Does thy life destroy.
                  (William Blake)

Reflect

Every rose faces death. Its crimson joy, its lush beauty, its attracting aroma are vulnerable to the worms of death and decay. On a stormy night, the worm crawls into bed with beauty. Joy confronts the dark mystery of death. How can human beings, except by way of great pretense, claim joy when all the while death sits smugly just around the corner? No one escapes the mystery of death. Mortality is built into the unmuted contract with life.

Joy hinges on the possibility that death leads to transformed life. After all, any flower or person experiences just so many nights and storms. Joy comes in believing and embracing death as transformation to new life. The Resurrection provides blessed assurance of this.

What are your personal experiences of crimson joy, joy that you associate with nights and storms, thorns and ants? Pray to savor crimson joys in your life right now.

Respond

Living God,
    heal our sickness and give us life.
May your gift of faith help us
    to see your plan of new life
    in the center of suffering and death.
Give us crimson joy,
    so that we might love those
    who face nights and storms.
Give us wisdom to know life's dark secrets.

26.

A Shadow of Comparison

Listen

The rare appearance of joy at work is so painfully exquisite that we may actually experience joy as a moment of terror. It opens to us all our possibilities and yet casts a shadow of comparison across all our other moments. Joy brings an intimation of death and mortality. This joy will pass as all others have before them. Laughter catches in our throat because we refuse to accept the corollary of joy, the soul-enriching poignancy of loss.

(David Whyte)

Reflect

Is it possible to take delight in doing the laundry, mowing the lawn, taking the deposition, scrubbing for surgery, plowing the field, filling out tax forms? If joy is impossible here, we are destined for large portions of sadness.

The incapacity for joy in work or play may well be grounded in our inability to embrace death and loss. Why get a dog for the kids when we know that in thirteen years or so it will be dead? Or, to go even farther, knowing the possibility of so much anguish and suffering in the world, why should we even have kids? Until we have the wisdom to see in loss and death a soul-enriching possibility, we will never live life to the full.

Back to work! Has your sense of mortality thrown too many shadows on your delight in life? Ponder and then list all the ways possible to bring to your work world, if not a deep enthusiasm for some specific task, at least a level of motivation that is grounded in love or the joy of sociability in being with others.

Respond

God of all life and holiness,
    grant us the wisdom to embrace
    the joys and griefs
    that come to us on our journey of faith.
Both in light and darkness you abide with us, and
    drive from our soul all terror and fear.
Strengthen us in living deeply
    whatever comes our way,
    knowing that your providential love
    holds us in being.

27.

Joy in All

Listen

There is joy
in all:
in the hair I brush each morning,
in the Cannon towel, newly washed,
that I rub my body with each morning,
in the chapel of eggs I cook
each morning,
in the outcry from the kettle
that heats my coffee
each morning,
in the spoon and the chair
that cry "hello there, Anne"
each morning,
in the godhead of the table
that I set my silver, plate, cup upon
each morning.

All this is God
right here in my pea-green house
each morning
and I mean,
though often forget,
to give thanks,
to faint down by the kitchen table

in a prayer of rejoicing
as the holy birds at the kitchen window
peck into their marriage of seeds.
So while I think of it,
let me paint a thank-you on my palm
for this God, this laughter of the morning,
lest it go unspoken.

The Joy that isn't shared, I've heard,
dies young.

(Anne Sexton)

Reflect

A statement heard somewhere long ago says, "A sense of gratitude is the only real source of joyful generosity." Attend to the kernel of joy residing in everything, even breakfast eggs, clean towels, fresh coffee, French toast. Ponder the relationship between the inseparable first cousins, joy and gratitude.

Respond

Creator of all things,
        today I rejoice and give you thanks for . . .

28.

Glad Instruments

Listen

To be glad instruments of God's love in this imperfect world is the service to which [people] are called, and it forms a preparatory stage to the bliss that awaits them in the perfected world, the Kingdom of God.

(Albert Schweitzer)

Reflect

The question of discovering one's vocation, one's calling in life, appears complex. Each individual has unique gifts, each age has its particular needs, each culture provides opportunities and imposes limits. Throw into the stew our gene pool, our convoluted family systems, the history of each nation, and discerning one's calling increases in difficulty. Yet, isn't there but one thing necessary on life's journey? We need but choose the better part that no one can take from us.

Albert Schweitzer formulates our universal calling as being "glad instruments of God's love," nothing more, nothing less. Throughout the centuries great philosophers and theologians, mystics and prophets come back to the single mystery of love—receiving this grace and giving it away. William Blake said it this way: "And we are put on earth a little space. / That we may learn to bear the beams of love." Once having borne the beams, we give them away. We become joyful instruments of God's love in a world fragile and imperfect.

How can you be a "glad instrument" of God's love today? Persevere in looking for and trying out even the smallest ways. At the end of the day, reflect on how you played your glad instrument.

Respond

God of love and peace,
    shape us into instruments
    of your presence in our fragile world.
We sometimes channel hatred and despair into
       the stream of life.
We sometimes are conduits of indifference
       and greed.
Call us to conversion, and form us into the image
       of your Son.
Then, embracing your call, we shall make present
       the power and joy of your love.
Then we shall be glad instruments of your Reign.

29.

Play's Intention

Listen

Joy is play's intention. When this intention is actually realized, in joyful play, the time structure of the playful universe takes on a very specific quality—namely, *it becomes eternity*. This is probably true of all experiences of intense joy, even when they are not enveloped in the separate reality of play. This is the final insight of Nietzsche's Zarathustra in the midnight song: "All joy wills eternity—wills deep, deep eternity."

(Peter L. Berger)

Reflect

Joy has a way of eliminating time. In the precious moment of ecstasy, the soul crosses over into the land of eternity, leaving time behind to nasty successiveness. Joy has no time for the past or future, but demands that the present be crowned with immortality. We need but watch children at play to witness this convergence of joy and eternity. Children are simply lost in the splendor of the story, the song, the building blocks, the movie. Vulnerable to being transported, they have not developed the "mature" habit of clinging to so many things. Children simply let go and slide down deep into the eternal joy of the now.

Why do people take pictures at moments of joy: the championship team, the newly married couple, the academic diploma held high? Are we not, with our photography, attempting to hold forever these moments of joy, yearning to prevent their slipping into the grave of mortality. Our bookshelves of albums confirm the thesis that joy wills eternity.

Revisit the photographs in your albums that manifest joy. What types of play bring you the deepest joy? Go, play.

Respond

On the seventh day, gracious God,
    you rested to take delight in your Creation.
That day became eternal at Christ's
    Resurrection.
May we experience the glory of the risen life,
    a life of eternal joy in the mystery of love.
Send your Spirit into our every moment
    thereby turning all time into eternity,
    all moments into play.

30.

Disproportionate Joy

Listen

I have often been able to be the bringer of joy to others; this in a country in which small things, small gifts, small recognitions, small identifications, can bring disproportionate joy.

(Alan Paton)

Reflect

Many countries on our planet are filled with sorrow and deep poverty. Hundreds of thousands of refugees travel without hope. In South Africa, a land in which Alan Paton lived and worked, generations of people suffered from apartheid and lived under the weight of oppression. To many of these people, Paton and others were bringers of joy.

Little things do mean a lot. A smile given to the despondent, a piece of bread offered to the hungry, a blanket covering another's nakedness and cold often result in disproportionate joy. Under different circumstances these meager gifts would hardly be acknowledged. In the land of joy and sorrow there is little proportionality.

The Spirit lets loose of its logic and restraint and tends to run riot. Surely it is the very disproportionality of joy that elicits our uncontrollable laughter. Surely it is the very disproportionality of our sorrow that throws us back into the arms of God's mercy.

Would you want the phrase "bringer of joy" etched on your tombstone? If so, what are you doing and how are you "being" so that you will deserve this epitaph?

Respond

Jesus, bringer of joy and peace,
    make us instruments of these gifts
    in our time.
Make us sensitive to the sorrow and distress of others. Fill us with your compassion,
    a compassion that lures us
    into active concern
    for others.
Teach us the beauty of disproportionate joy.

31.

Like a Dance

Listen

A good relationship has a pattern like a dance and is built on some of the same rules. . . . The joy of such a pattern is not only the joy of creation or the joy of participation, it is also the joy of living in the moment. Lightness of touch and living in the moment are intertwined. One cannot dance well unless one is completely in time with the music, not leaning back to the last step or pressing forward to the next one, but poised directly on the present step as it comes. Perfect poise on the beat is what gives good dancing its sense of ease, of timelessness, of the eternal. It is what Blake was speaking of when he wrote:

> *He who bends to himself a joy*
> *Doth the winged life destroy;*
> *But he who kisses the joy as it flies*
> *Lives in Eternity's sunrise.*
> (Anne Morrow Lindbergh)

Reflect

Dancing is an excellent metaphor for the spiritual life. God takes the initiative in leading us through the various phrases of our life. Our task is to respond faithfully to the slightest impulse and drawing, keenly aware that the pattern is always one of love and union. Herein lies our joy: to embrace the present moment with our whole being.

Our God is the Lord of the dance. We are invited into the divine movement and spend most of our lifetime attempting to learn the beat. When we finally get it, there is indeed a sense of ease, a sense of timelessness, a sense of eternity. At last there is a sense of joy.

How are you dancing with God? Are you dancing as a willing partner? Close your eyes and recall moments when life was a dance, when the moment delighted you and became aglow with joy. Do you need to let go of anything so that you can dance more?

Respond

Lord of the dance,
>	may we learn the music of your heart,
>	and may we participate in the movements
>	of your grace.
Draw us into the human family
>	that we might share deeply the whole of life.
May your Spirit fill us with the sound
>	of your music,
>	and may we find joy in the doing of your will.

Acknowledgments

The psalms cited in this book are from *Psalms Anew: In Inclusive Language,* compiled by Nancy Schreck and Maureen Leach (Winona, MN: Saint Mary's Press, 1986). Copyright © 1986 by Saint Mary's Press. All rights reserved.

The scriptural quotation on page 44 is from the *Good News Bible*. Copyright © 1966, 1971, 1976 by the American Bible Society. All rights reserved.

All other scriptural quotations in this book are from the *New Revised Standard Version of the Bible*. Copyright © 1989 by the Division of Christian Education of the National Council of the Churches of Christ in the United States of America. All rights reserved.

The excerpt on page 8 is from *The Diary of a Country Priest*, by Georges Bernanos, translated by Pamela Morris (New York: Macmillan Company, 1937), page 236. Copyright © 1937 by Macmillan Company.

The excerpts from the poem, "The Little Black Boy," on pages 8 and 64 by William Blake are from *The Poems of William Blake*, edited by W. H. Stevenson (London: Longman Group Limited, 1971), page 58. Copyright © 1971 by Longman Group Limited.

The excerpt on page 9 from Patrice J. Tuohy's interview with Thea Bowman is from "Sister Thea Bowman: On the Road to Glory," *U.S. Catholic* (June 1990): pages 21–26.

The excerpt on page 10 by Thérèse of Lisieux is from *Story of a Soul: The Autobiography of St. Thérèse of Lisieux*, translated by John Clarke, OCD (Washington, DC: Institute of Carmelite Studies Publications, 1976), page 137. Copyright © 1972 by Editions du Cerf et Desclée de Brouwer. Translation copyright © 1975, 1976 by Washington Province of Discalced Carmelites.

The excerpt from the poem on page 20, "God's Grandeur," by Gerard Manley Hopkins is from *A Hopkins Reader*, selected by John Pick (New York: Oxford University Press, 1953), page 13. Copyright © 1953 by Oxford University Press. Used with permission.